TO: _____

FROM: _____

D1091961

90 DAY DEVOTIONAL

# WINTER

### A
### SEASON
### OF
### CELEBRATION

**BroadStreet**
PUBLISHING

BroadStreet Publishing Group LLC
Racine, Wisconsin, USA
Broadstreetpublishing.com

# WINTER: A Season of Celebration

© 2017 by BroadStreet Publishing

ISBN: 978-1-4245-5576-5

Devotional entries compiled by Michelle Winger.

Design by Chris Garborg | garborgdesign.com
Edited by Michelle Winger | literallyprecise.com

Printed in China.

17  18  19  20  21  22  23      7  6  5  4  3  2  1

The rain and the snow
come down from heaven,
and do not return to it
without watering the earth
and making it bud
and flourish.

ISAIAH 55:10 NIV

# INTRODUCTION

Winter. It's a season of celebration. A season
of beauty and anticipation. A season of
snowflakes and scarves, and watching flames
dance in the fireplace.

We spend time enhancing relationships
with family and friends, sharing meals and
attending parties. We exchange smiles with
strangers and gifts with loved ones.

This 90-day devotional will encourage you
to spend some time with God, celebrating
the gift of his Son. Experience his life,
joy, and peace during the busyness of the
celebration season.

# WINTER TREASURES

*The day is yours, and yours also the night;*
*you established the sun and moon.*
*It was you who set all the boundaries of the earth;*
*you made both summer and winter.*

PSALM 74:16-17 NIV

Those who live in a cold climate understand that winters can get long. As the amount of daylight decreases, it's easy to find discouragement or depression creeping in. Sometimes this is a direct result of just needing more vitamin D to compensate for the lack of sunlight. But sometimes the Lord allows this to drive you to a place of finding a deeper degree of contentment in him.

God created the seasons. They are his making. Winter treasures are like manna—the same manna would be rotten in the summer. Manna that is provided on a daily basis refreshes us and provides the kind of nourishment we need.

Collect the winter manna you need to get through today. God has more than enough blessing to pour it out again tomorrow.

*What is your winter manna? What word is God speaking
to you in this season?*

God, help me to make the most out of this season. I don't want
to live in complaint or wish away the winter. There are treasures
to be found in this place that I don't want to miss.

# COME AWAY

*My beloved speaks and says to me:*
*"Arise, my love, my beautiful one, and come away,*
*for behold, the winter is past; the rain is over and gone.*
*The flowers appear on the earth, the time of singing has come."*

SONG OF SOLOMON 2:10-12 ESV

Some say that romance is dead. It's not for God: the lover of our souls. He desires nothing more than time with his creation! It can be a little uncomfortable to have his gaze so intently upon us though. We're nothing special, after all! Not beauty queens, academic scholars, or athletic prodigies of any kind. We might not be musical, or crafty, or organized. Our house might be a mess, and we could probably use a manicure.

Do you feel a bit squeamish under such an adoring gaze? There is good news for you! You are, in fact, his beautiful one! And he does, indeed, want to bring you out of the cold winter. He's finished the watering season and it is finally—*finally*—time to rejoice in the season of renewal.

*How do you feel under the gaze of the Almighty God?*
*Don't be ashamed; he loves you dearly.*

Heavenly Father, I don't know why I feel uncomfortable under
your gaze. You love me more than anyone else ever could!
Regardless of how unworthy I think I am, I want to rise up and
come away with you.

# PERFECT FRIEND

*"Here I am! I stand at the door and knock. If anyone hears
my voice and opens the door, I will come in and eat with
that person, and they with me."*

REVELATION 3:20 NIV

God created you for relationship with him just as he created
Adam and Eve. He delights in your voice, your laughter, and your
ideas. He longs to fellowship with you. When life gets difficult, do
you run to him with your frustrations? When you're overwhelmed
with sadness or grief, do you carry your pain to him? In the heat of
anger or frustration, do you call on him for freedom? He is a friend
that offers all of this to us—and more—in mercy and love. He is
worthy of our friendship.

The friendship he offers to us is a gift of immeasurable worth.
There is no one like him; indeed, there is none as worthy of our
fellowship than God Almighty, our Maker and Redeemer. Train
your heart to run first to God with your pain, joy, frustration, and
excitement. His friendship will never let you down!

*How is God better than any friend you could ever have?*

God, you are the perfect friend. If I think of all I need in a
friendship, I know that I can find it in you. Thank you that your
friendship surpasses all of my expectations.

# WALK STEADY

*Direct my footsteps according to your word;*
*let no sin rule over me.*

PSALM 119:133 NIV

What is it about high heels? Every family album contains a photo of an adorable toddler attempting to walk in Mama's shoes, and every woman remembers her first wobbly attempt to appear graceful in that first pair of pumps. How did she make it look so easy, so elegant? Most of us also have a memory of a not-so-graceful stumble or even a twisted ankle; yet, somehow the stiletto retains its appeal. Who hasn't relied on the steady arm of an escort or companion in far more sensible footwear?

Walking with Jesus is a little like learning to walk in four-inch heels. Others make it look so easy, gliding along apparently sinless while we feel shaky and uncertain, prone to stumble at any moment. Will we take a wrong step? Fall flat on our faces? (Do anyone else's feet hurt?)

*In which aspect of your walk do you feel the most steady and certain? The least? Share your confidence and your concerns with the Savior, and invite him to lead you in both.*

I lean on your strong arm today, my Savior;
steady me and direct my steps.

# FOLLOW THE ARROW

*Your ears shall hear a word behind you, saying,*
*"This is the way, walk in it,"*
*Whenever you turn to the right hand*
*or whenever you turn to the left."*

ISAIAH 30:21 NKJV

Decisions, decisions. It seems a week never goes by without
our needing to make at least one important choice. Whether
job related, relationship motivated, or something as seemingly
innocent as how to spend a free Friday, wouldn't it be nice to have
an arrow pointing us in the right direction—especially if we are in
danger of making a wrong turn?

According to God's Word, we have exactly that. When we truly
desire to walk the path God sets us on, and when we earnestly seek
his voice, he promises to lead us in the right direction. His ever-
present Spirit is right there, ready to put us back on the path each
time we wander off.

*Consider the decisions before you right now. Who are you
turning to for guidance? Lay your options before God,
and then listen for his voice.*

God, I come to you today and ask for your wisdom. I want to be
led by you. You know the path that is best suited to fulfill your
plan for my life. Help me to be obedient to you as you show me
which way to go.

# THE WRITING
# ON THE WALL

*I will be careful to live an innocent life.*
*When will you come to me?*
*I will live an innocent life in my house.*
*I will not look at anything wicked.*
*I hate those who turn against you;*
*they will not be found near me.*
*Let those who want to do wrong stay away from me;*
*I will have nothing to do with evil.*

PSALM 101:2-4 NCV

What types of messages do we allow to enter our homes on a daily basis through television, social media, internet, magazines, smartphones, or even our own conversations? Do we take the time to really ponder and evaluate the ideas that we absorb even subconsciously?

Let the messages in your home be messages of godliness. Let your loved ones see and hear the words of life and truth above those of sin and death. Choose carefully the words and images that enter your home and your heart.

*Print some of your favorite verses out
and hang them on your walls.*

**H**oly Spirit, you are my greatest ally when determining which messages I should or should not allow into my home. Help me to listen to your prompting, and not ignore you when you gently tell me that something isn't healthy for my spirit.

# BELIEVE HE IS GOOD

*Adam was not the one deceived; it was the woman who was deceived and became a sinner.*

1 TIMOTHY 2:14 NIV

Eve, the mother of all, changed humanity forever when she made one fatal decision to venture outside God's boundaries. When she took a bite of the forbidden fruit, she did more than just give in to her own desire for pleasure, she opened the door of sin to every generation that would follow after her.

Eve's key mistake was that she doubted the goodness of God. The serpent knew he could penetrate a woman's mind with well-spoken words, and he convinced Eve that God was withholding something from her. As she believed that God was depriving her, she also believed that God wasn't good after all—that he didn't have her best interest at heart. The moment Eve stopped believing God was good was the moment that temptation overcame her.

*How often do you doubt the goodness of God? Do you wonder if the boundaries he's put in place are really necessary or right? Do you doubt that God really cares about the details of your life?*

I choose to remember today, God, that you are good, and that I can trust you completely.

# THE COST OF
# SACRIFICE

*However, the king said to Araunah, "No, but I will surely*
*buy it from you for a price, for I will not offer burnt offerings*
*to the Lord my God which cost me nothing." So David bought*
*the threshing floor and the oxen for fifty shekels of silver.*

2 SAMUEL 24:24 NASB

What are you not doing right now because of fear? Are there
things you are keeping quiet about simply because you're afraid?
Are there steps forward that you aren't taking because you're
frightened about what may happen if you do? Are there stirrings in
your heart that you're neglecting because you're afraid of how you
may be criticized?

In the Bible, when God announced what he was about to do in
someone's life, he often began it with the words, "Do not fear." He
knew we would worry. He knew we would list the cons and stress
over the details, and he said don't.

*What are you holding back from God? In light of what his death cost him, is there really a price too high for your sacrifice to him?*

Jesus, thank you for dying on the cross and paying the price for my life—not for my money or for my talents. You don't just want the parts of me that others see, you want the secret, hidden part of my heart. Help me to openly show that to you, knowing that you can see it anyway.

# YOU ARE CHERISHED

*I am convinced that neither death nor life, neither angels nor demons, neither the present nor the future, nor any powers, neither height nor depth, nor anything else in all creation, will be able to separate us from the love of God that is in Christ Jesus our Lord.*

ROMANS 8:38-39 NIV

What feeling really compares to knowing someone has run through the rain, cancelled an international flight, driven all night—for you? Even if we've never experienced it, we've imagined it in our hearts.

Maybe we've had the realization that we, too, would move heaven and earth for the one we love the most. Whether husband, child, parent, sibling, or dear friend, to love and be loved deeply just may be the best feeling there is.

How much love you have given or received is a mere sampling of the way Jesus feels about you.

*Let these incredible words above wash over you
as you realize there is nothing—absolutely nothing—
Jesus wouldn't do for you.*

Father, thank you for showing me that I am cherished, loved
beyond reason or measure. You really can move heaven and
earth, and you would do so in a heartbeat—for me.

# A "YES" FAITH

*Abram believed the Lord. And the Lord accepted Abram's faith, and that faith made him right with God.*

GENESIS 15:6 NCV

Have you ever stepped out and said yes to something crazy for God? You followed him into the middle of the ocean and trusted him to keep you afloat. Stepping out in faith isn't easy. In fact, it's messy. It's a lot of wondering what you're doing, and why you're doing it. Of closing your eyes and begging God to remind you of the things he placed on your heart when he originally gave you the vision.

When you stand in the truth that you have obeyed, it doesn't really matter how everything looks or feels. What matters is that you were obedient. You believed what God was telling you.

Stepping out in faith is about boldly facing your harshest critics and telling them you're not sure if everything will work out. It's being at peace in total chaos. It's putting yourself out there and wondering if you'll live up to expectation. It's wondering if you have anything to offer after all.

*If God is asking you to do something that terrifies you,*
*step out in faith. Obey him. Believe him. It will be worth it.*

God, there is peace in obedience—peace that even when I'm criticized, laughed at, and misunderstood, you are pleased. Everything else fades away in light of that awesome reality.

# A WARM WELCOME

*Accept one another, then, just as Christ accepted you,
in order to bring praise to God.*

ROMANS 15:7 NIV

Have you ever met someone and immediately felt a connection?
Maybe you were drawn to their personality and a friendship was
born. Have you ever met someone you struggled to connect with?
Maybe the way they dressed, acted, talked, or chose their career
was completely foreign to you.

We all have our natural friendships. We don't have to be best
friends with everyone we meet because the truth of it is, we won't.
But what if, despite our differences, we still accepted all those we
come in contact with?

*Strive today to accept those around you and to genuinely welcome them with open arms in spite of your differences.*

God, as your follower, my main goal is to bring you praise.
I know I need to accept others with the same measure of
absolute acceptance that you extend to me.
Help me to do this well so I bring honor to you.

# EMOTIONS

*Is anyone among you suffering? Let him pray.*
*Is anyone cheerful? Let him sing praise.*

JAMES 5:13 ESV

It is no secret that women can be emotional. We are complicated creatures who feel deeply. Sometimes our emotions make us feel like a bit of a mess, so we try to hide them from those around us—and even from God.

God created us to live with a full range of emotions. He is aware how those feelings directly impact our daily lives. God is not frustrated with us as we feel all of the things that he created us to feel. He is not offended by our anger, impatient with our tears, or bothered by our laughter.

*Don't be tempted to come to God with your emotions covered up. Allow him to see your raw emotion in all its honesty.*

Father, I lay everything before you, holding nothing back. I know you love me and you will stick with me through good times and bad. Thank you.

# APPETITE

*"No one can serve two masters; for a slave will either hate the one and love the other, or be devoted to the one and despise the other. You cannot serve God and wealth."*

MATTHEW 6:24 NRSV

Appetite is a funny thing. Our bodies have the ability to communicate hunger to our brains, and our brains then cause us to seek out a solution to the problem. When we are genuinely hungry, we look for food that will fill our stomachs and quiet our hunger.

Our souls have appetites also, but we so easily fill our time and energy with the world's entertainment. We fill ourselves up with things that will never be able to satisfy and leave little room for the only one who can.

There is a throne in your heart upon which only one master can sit—and you must choose wisely who will take residence there.

*Will you allow your life to be ruled by the pursuit of things which will never last, or will you accept nothing less than eternal stock for your life's investment?*

God, I want you to be on the throne of my heart.
I want to be ruled by the pursuit of eternal life with you.

# NO CONDEMNATION

*Straightening up, Jesus said to her, "Woman, where are they? Did no one condemn you?" She said, "No one, Lord." And Jesus said, "I do not condemn you either. Go. From now on sin no more."*

JOHN 8:10-11 NASB

Most of us know the story of the woman caught in adultery. One of the intriguing moments was when Jesus was questioned about whether or not the woman should be stoned. His response is to stoop down and start writing in the dirt. Jesus' action of stooping in the dirt literally defines one interpretation of the word *grace*.

As they all stood casting judgement, Jesus removed himself from the accusers, stooping low and occupying himself elsewhere. It spoke volumes about his lack of participation in the crowd's judgement. Because of Jesus' distraction, the eyes of the onlookers were drawn off the woman, perhaps lifting a portion of her shame. With their attention focused on Jesus, he said the words that saved the woman's life: "Let him who has never sinned cast the first stone." One by one, the accusers walked away.

Jesus was the only one qualified to stone the adulterous woman. This is a beautiful foreshadowing of the redemption he later brought to all sinners.

*Jesus is the only one qualified to condemn you, and he chose to condemn himself instead. You are free and clean because of the grace of Jesus Christ.*

Jesus, that you extend your grace to me time and time again blows my mind. I cannot fathom everything that you went through to make me clean and whole. Thank you for not condemning me and for setting me free.

# CONTINUAL PRAISE

*I will praise the L*ORD *at all times;*
*his praise is always on my lips.*

PSALM 34:1 NCV

It's relatively easy to sing God's praises when all is going well in our lives: when he blesses us with something we asked for, when he heals us, or when he directly answers a prayer. We naturally turn and give him praise and glory for good things. What about when things aren't going well? What about in dry times, painful times, or times of waiting?

Do we only praise God for something after he's given it, or do we praise him ahead of time in faith, knowing that he will always be good no matter what happens? We should look at all difficulties in life as miracles waiting to happen—chances for God to show his goodness and bring us closer to his heart.

*Choose today to have praise readily on your lips instead of complaint. Whenever you feel discontentment or frustration, replace it with praise.*

Father, I choose to focus on your goodness today. I know this will increase my joy and lessen the pain of the hardships I am enduring. Give me strength to continue to praise you.

# A LOVE THAT IS FELT

*"These people come near to me with their mouth*
*and honor me with their lips,*
*but their hearts are far from me.*
*Their worship of me is based on merely*
*human rules they have been taught."*

ISAIAH 29:13 NIV

Think about the most romantic movie you've ever seen. Two beautiful people portray an even more beautiful love on the silver screen, taking your heart on a romantic adventure as they play out passion right before your eyes. But behind the camera, do those two people really feel that love? They are actors. They are good at what they do. They can make that love story look so very real.

Is love really love when given outwardly but not felt inwardly? Even though it may look to everyone around you that you are passionately in love, if that love is not genuine in your heart, then it's not love at all.

*If our worship is borne out of true love and intimacy, it will go much further than the outward displays of affection.*

God, your love permeates my heart and my life. I don't want to just look like someone in love, I want to actually be someone who is in love with you.

# PREPARED TO SERVE

*"Very truly, I tell you, the Son can do nothing on his own,
but only what he sees the Father doing; for whatever the
Father does, the Son does likewise. The Father loves the Son
and shows him all that he himself is doing; and he will show
him greater works than these, so that you will be astonished."*

JOHN 5:19-20 NRSV

A natural response to feeling the love of God is to want to do
things for him. But we have to become people of God before we
can effectively do God's work. The only way to become his people
is to spend time in his presence.

The disciples didn't go directly from responding to God's call to full
time, full blown ministry. They spent a lot of time with Jesus first—
learning from him, talking with him, and watching him minister.

*Not even Jesus acted without first paying attention to what God was saying. Take time to be quiet before God and ponder his words and his plans.*

Through knowing your heart, God, I will discover where you are already working. I want to join you in your will. Give me wisdom to make the right choices that will lead me there.

# GIVING THANKS

*Open for me the Temple gates.*
*Then I will come in and thank the LORD.*
*This is the LORD's gate;*
*only those who are good may enter through it.*

PSALM 118:19-20 NCV

What happens in our souls when we say thank you to God? When we consecrate a passing second by breathing gratitude into it? What happens to our very being when we acknowledge the weight and glory of even the most insignificant gift?

With each moment of paused reflection, each thank-filled statement, we are set free. Set free from negativity. Set free from dark thoughts of death, pain, suffering, and ugliness. We enter his gates with thanksgiving. We enter his holy place. We walk directly through the door he created.

To walk in thanksgiving is to walk right into God's presence.

*Practice saying thank you today—knowing that through your thankfulness, you will usher yourself into the presence of God.*

God, this season of thanksgiving has a way of taking my heart and righting it. It opens my eyes to wonder and splendor in casual moments. It puts things into perspective and restores triumph to my defeated soul. Thank you!

# REJOICE, PRAY, THANK

*Rejoice always; pray without ceasing; in everything give thanks; for this is God's will for you in Christ Jesus.*

1 Thessalonians 5:16-18 NASB

It is easy for us to get weighed down with the negative things in this world. Our lives, and the lives of those around us, are full of troubles that make us weary. Some days it can be difficult to find joy in the midst of our own chaos.

We wonder what God's will is, especially in the hardships. We can't see his master plan, but feel as though if we could, maybe we could make it through. We wonder what God wants us to do in the middle of our difficulties.

These three things: constant rejoicing, prayer, and thanksgiving are the formula for doing God's will in our lives.

*Throughout the day, think about what you're thankful for.*

God, I rejoice continually in what you have done for me.
I want to thank you intentionally for your blessings today.

# SIN ERASED

*The next day he saw Jesus coming toward him and declared,
"Here is the Lamb of God who takes away
the sin of the world!"*

JOHN 1:29 NRSV

When we step into the holy presence of God, our sin becomes obvious. We feel the separation and shame that our mistakes have built. There is nothing we can do to eliminate our sin and restore our connection to the living God. We need a solution and we have none.

When Adam and Eve sinned and discovered their nakedness, God killed a young lamb and clothed them with it. In this action, God set the monumental precedent that the blood of an innocent lamb covers sin. The blood of the Lamb, Jesus Christ, would be shed on the cross centuries later to cover the sin of all mankind.

Nothing is hidden from God's sight. He knows your sin, he knows your shame, and he knows your predicament. But he made the sacrifice demanded for your sin. Jesus shed his own blood, and that blood covers your sin.

*Rest in his unfailing love for you and in his power
to take away your sin.*

Jesus, all of my shame, all of my errors, all of my unworthiness is
erased by the work you have already done. I am so grateful.

# THE SACRIFICE OF THANKSGIVING

*Offer to God a sacrifice of thanksgiving*
*Call upon Me in the day of trouble;*
*I shall rescue you, and you will honor Me.*

PSALM 50:14-15 NASB

The Israelites in the Old Testament had a complicated list of rituals and sacrifices to follow. Among the five special offerings, one was the peace offering, or the sacrifice of thanksgiving. God asked that an animal without defect be offered to him from a heart that was full of gratitude for his grace. When Jesus came, the old requirements were replaced by the new so that our worship could be an expression of our hearts directly through our lips.

It's not always easy to be thankful. In times of great difficulty when everything in the natural screams "I don't like this!" gratitude comes at great sacrifice. It is a denial of the natural response, dying to one's own preference, and in submission saying, "God, your way is best and I thank you." Having a grateful heart gives us the privilege of calling on God in our day of trouble and the assurance of his deliverance.

*How can you offer God your sacrifice of praise today?*

Lord, today I want to say thanks for being my God and for the grace you show me each day. As I call out to you, I know you will be my deliverer and get all the glory in the process!

# TELL THE STORY

*Jesus constantly used these illustrations when speaking to the crowds. In fact, because the prophets said that he would use so many, he never spoke to them without at least one illustration. For it had been prophesied, "I will talk in parables; I will explain mysteries hidden since the beginning of time."*

MATTHEW 13:34-35 TLB

We enjoy listening to stories because they help us to relate with a concept and personalize an idea. We hear a lofty explanation and struggle to understand, but a story illustrates the same thought and we become connected to it.

Jesus was a storyteller. While he walked the earth, he told people many stories in order to teach them something. Jesus used parables and imagery instead of "just spitting it out" so that people would meditate, speculate, study, and absorb the words to better understand them.

When people who don't know God hear the Gospel, it can be confusing because their eyes have not been opened by the Holy Spirit. When you share with them your own story of God's work in your life, their hearts and minds may be more easily opened.

Jesus, the parables you told weren't just simple stories; their symbolisms revealed secrets of your heavenly kingdom, and made its glory digestible for the common man. Thank you for sharing those secrets with us!

# BEAUTIFUL
# GIRLHOOD

*Let their flesh be renewed like a child's;*
*let them be restored as in the days of their youth—*
*then that person can pray to God and find favor with him,*
*they will see God's face and shout for joy;*
*he will restore them to full well-being.*

JOB 33:25-26 NIV

Close your eyes for a moment and think back to when you were a little girl. Do you see her? What is she like? Excitable? Passionate? Quiet? Shy? Remember for a moment what it was like to be that little girl: caring nothing of dirty hands or mussed-up hair. Caring only for that moment—the fleeting moment of freedom and unpredictability. A girl who can lose herself in make believe and dreams. A girl who knows how to dance wildly and run freely. A girl who knows full well the arts of day dreaming and wild flower picking.

That little girl grew up quickly, didn't she? Responsibility eventually overtakes carefree spontaneity. Reality drowns out limitless dreams. Restoration of full well-being can be ours! Doesn't that sound just like childhood? Beloved, God can restore to you what's been lost.

*What life has threatened to strip from you,*
*God can restore and reshape.*

God, I choose to forget today about the things which never really mattered all that much, and I remember instead what it is to breathe life in my lungs. Thank you for each breath.

# WHEN YOUR HEART IS TROUBLED

*"Peace I leave with you; my peace I give you. I do not give to you as the world gives. Do not let your hearts be troubled and do not be afraid."*

JOHN 14:27 NIV

*I can't get a moment's peace.* Sound familiar? We all go through seasons where it seems every corner hides a new challenge to our serenity, assuming we've actually achieved any semblance of serenity in the first place. Why is it so hard to find peace in this world? Because we're looking *in this world.*

After his resurrection, before Jesus ascended into heaven, he left his disciples with something they'd never had before: peace. More specifically, he gave them his peace, a gift not of this world. Whatever the world can offer us can also be taken from us. Any security, happiness, or temporary reprieve from suffering is just that: temporary. Only the things of heaven are permanent and cannot be taken away.

"Do not let your heart be troubled," Jesus tells us. This means we have a choice. Share the things with him that threaten your peace, and then remember they have no hold on you.

God, I am yours, and your peace is mine. Thank you.

# WE HAVE TIME

*Be careful how you live. Don't live like fools, but like those who are wise. Make the most of every opportunity in these evil days. Don't act thoughtlessly, but understand what the Lord wants you to do.*

EPHESIANS 5:15-17 NLT

Time is one of those things we never seem to have enough of. Many of our days can feel like a race against the clock to get everything done. We seem to lack the time we need for even the most important things—things like being in God's Word, spending intentional time with loved ones, or volunteering to help those in need.

At the end of the day, there is one reality we must remember: we have time for what we make time for. It's easy to feel busy, but what are we truly busying ourselves with? Are we finding time to spend browsing social media or watching re-runs of our favorite TV shows? Are we finding time to take a long shower or sleep for a few extra minutes in the morning? None of those things are necessarily wrong, but if we feel pressed for time and unable to spend time with the Lord, we may need to rethink where our time goes.

*Take a good hard look at your day today and think about
how you can spend your time most wisely.*

Father, I want to live my life in a way that makes the most
of the moments and opportunities you have laid before me.
Teach me to be careful with my time and energy.

# ENCOURAGEMENT IN GOD'S WORD

*O LORD, I have longed for your rescue,*
*and your instructions are my delight.*
*Let me live so I can praise you,*
*and may your regulations help me.*

PSALM 119:174-175 NLT

There is wonder to be found in snowflakes, raindrops, and even strange bugs. Though we often don't love the idea of encountering too many of any one of those, if we stop and look, if we allow ourselves to really *see* what is there, it's pretty amazing.

The same can be true of God's Word. It may be displayed in various forms and places throughout our homes, schools, work places, or church buildings, but if we don't stop to really drink in the words that are there, we can miss the rich blessing behind them. When we believe that God wants to encourage us through his Word, we will no doubt find encouragement in it—because God intended it to be used for that purpose!

*Find an encouraging word that you love in the Scriptures today and write it down for daily reflection.*

God, help me not to gloss over the beauty and depth of your Word. Only your Word carries the richness of eternity and the encouragement I need for each new day.

# HE IS FAITHFUL

*Your faithfulness extends to every generation,
as enduring as the earth you created.*

PSALM 119:90 NLT

What's the oldest thing you own? How long have you had it, and what does it mean to you? Whether a decades-old diamond ring, twenty-year-old car, or a tattered baby blanket hanging together by threads, you probably know it won't last forever. How about your longest relationship? How many years have you been connected to this person through the good and the bad? One way we decide where to place our faith is longevity. History matters.

Consider now what God made: the earth we live on. Scientists estimate it to be 4.5 billion years old, give or take fifty million. Whether we think it's been around that long or six to ten thousand years, it's some quality workmanship. If we're looking for someone to trust, we won't find better credentials than that.

*Ponder all God has made and all he has done,*
*and share your heart with him regarding his faithfulness.*
*Have you embraced it?*

God, through every storm, every disaster, every war, and every
attack of the enemy, your creation still stands. Help me to
remember who I can depend on… forever.

# CONFIDENT IN INCOMPETENCE

*It is not that we think we are qualified to do anything on our own. Our qualification comes from God.*

2 CORINTHIANS 3:5 NLT

Whether bringing a brand new baby home from the hospital, giving your first major presentation at work, or simply making your first Thanksgiving meal, there's probably been at least one moment in your life that had you thinking, *I have no idea what I'm doing. I'm not qualified.* So what did you do? Chances are, you put a smile on your face, dove in, and did your best.

The older we get, the more we realize how truly helpless we are. We also, beautifully, realize it's okay. There is great freedom in admitting our shortcomings and allowing the Father to be our strength. No matter what he asks of us, we are confident in our incompetence.

*What dream or calling would you be able to fulfill if you were to embrace God's competence as your own?*

God, I may not be capable, but you are more than qualified to carry out your plans through me. Help me to swallow my pride and let you lead me.

# THE BURNING BUSH

*"When forty years had passed, an Angel of the Lord appeared to him in a flame of fire in a bush, in the wilderness of Mount Sinai."*

ACTS 7:30 NKJV

Do you ever feel like your life is in a holding pattern? Like your "something big" must be lurking around the next corner. You may feel like your life is being wasted while you wait for your own destiny.

God had Moses in a very similar holding pattern. He had this incredible experience at birth where he was specifically saved from certain death, miraculously found by the most powerful woman in the land, and raised as royalty. He had an unbelievable launch to his life, and then, after a fatal mistake, he became your average sheep herder in the desert for the next forty years. *Forty years.* That's a long time to wonder if the greatness of the vision you were born into will ever come to fruition.

The most amazing part of Moses' story, is that after all the waiting, God came to him in one of the most famous ways in history—and we all know how incredibly God went on to use Moses after that.

*Remember, if you feel directionless right now—without vision and without destiny—know that no wilderness is too remote for you to stumble upon a burning bush.*

Thank you, God, for your amazing way of showing up when I need you, and when you are trying to get my attention. I want to trust, to watch, and to wait for you to do something incredible with me.

# HOPE

*May the God of hope fill you with all joy and peace as you trust in him, so that you may overflow with hope by the power of the Holy Spirit.*

Romans 15:13 niv

What differentiates hope from a wish? Think about the lottery. Does one hope to win, or wish to win? How about a promotion, a pregnancy, or a proposal? Both hoping and wishing contain desire, but for wishing, that is where it ends. Hope goes deeper. The strong desire for something good to happen is coupled with a reason to believe that it will.

We see then how vital hope is, and why it's such a beautiful gift. Desire without hope is empty, but together they bring joy, expectancy, and peace. When we put our hope in Christ, he becomes our reason to believe good things will happen. He is our hope.

*Allow today's blessing from Romans to wash over you
as the Holy Spirit fills you with hope, joy, and peace.*

Father, I believe good things will happen in my life.
I have wonderful reason to believe this—
because my hope in in you, and you are good.

# TRUE RELIGION

*Pure and undefiled religion in the sight of our God and Father is this: to visit orphans and widows in their distress, and to keep oneself unstained by the world.*

JAMES 1:27 NASB

True religion— the kind that is acceptable to God—is found in giving ourselves to those who need the most. It's not about our comfort, our happiness, or even our ticket to heaven. It's about reflecting the glory of Christ on the earth.

The tender Father heart of God is far more interested in developing your love and Christ-like character than he is in keeping you comfortable. His compassion and intense love for mankind will not be satisfied with comfortable, cushioned Christianity.

*If you want to bring praise to God, intentionally seek out situations where you can put into practice your undefiled religion.*

God, I want to make it my mission to meet needs, to love, and to bring life. I know you want this too, and I can't do it without you. Give me your love for others so I have plenty to draw from.

# HUMILITY

*Humility is the fear of the LORD;*
*its wages are riches and honor and life*

PROVERBS 22:4 NIV

God values humility over pride and earthly success. That is why sometimes God makes us wait before revealing his plans for us. In the waiting is where he grows us in humility. When things don't work out perfectly, our pride is dismantled and we learn the most valuable lessons.

God being glorified in our lives doesn't make sense to our humanity because his plan isn't our plan and his ways are different. The entire message of the Gospel is upside-down from what we know here on earth. In God's kingdom, humility is elevated and pride is made low. Those who are poor are rich, and those who are weak are strong.

God is more concerned with having your heart fully devoted to him than he is with you having a successful ministry.

*Humble yourself in God's presence today.*

God, I know you want me to serve you and you love when
I prosper in kingdom work, but these are not your main goals.
You really just want to be with me forever. I am so blessed
and humbled by that.

# REDEEMED AND FREE

*The Spirit of the LORD is upon me,*
*because he has anointed me*
*to proclaim good news to the poor.*
*He has sent me to proclaim liberty to the captives*
*and recovering of sight to the blind,*
*to set at liberty those who are oppressed,*
*to proclaim the year of the LORD's favor.*

ISAIAH 61:1-2 ESV

When Jesus, the long-awaited Messiah, revealed his deity to his family, his disciples, and the crowds, they were expecting a mighty king who would deliver them from their oppressors and establish his everlasting kingdom. What they got was a humble servant who dined with tax collectors and whose feet were cleansed by the tears of a prostitute. Jesus wasn't exactly what they thought he would be.

*He was better!* He came to bring salvation to those who were drowning in a sea of sin and sickness; those who were cast out and in need of holy redemption; those whom the religious leaders had deemed unworthy but whose hearts longed for true restoration. He came to redeem his people, but not in the way they expected.

*How do you think people's expectations of the Messiah
made it difficult to accept him when he came?*

Jesus, you delivered me from the bonds of sin and oppression
through your death and resurrection. I praise you for my
freedom! Holy Spirit, rest upon me and give me boldness
to speak to others about this good news.

# TRADITIONS

*Stand firm and hold to the traditions that you were taught by us, either by our spoken word or by our letter.*

2 THESSALONIANS 2:15 ESV

Traditions are great. Those kinds of memories bind our hearts together whether it's bike rides down the beach, particular foods that you serve because Grandma used to make them, or having blueberry muffins by candlelight for the first day of school. But those traditions are even better when they impact our faith.

Maybe you read the Christmas story together on Christmas Eve, perhaps you pray together on New Year's Eve asking for God's blessings for the year ahead.

The important thing is that we pay attention to those events that have shaped us as Christians. Those will help us stand firm in our faith and strengthen our relationship with God.

*What spiritual traditions do you have already?*
*What new traditions could you implement?*

Father, thank you for the elements of faith that were
planted in me. Help me to stand firm in my faith.

# THE RIGHT REST

*"My Presence will go with you,*
*and I will give you rest."*

EXODUS 33:14 NIV

Women tend to be expert multitaskers. They juggle many responsibilities, schedules, and details. As the holiday season approaches, these tasks only seem to increase. Between the cooking and decorating, the parties and festivities—they can easily get tired out.

God says in his Word, "Be still and know that I am God." He asks us to stop, to sit, and rest because he designed us to need rest. There is a reason God set the example by resting on the seventh day after he made the world. Even the Creator knew the importance of rest.

*Have you ever gotten up from the couch and still felt weary—
sometimes even wearier than when you sat down? Don't
confuse resting your body with resting your soul. True life-
giving rest comes only from being in the presence of the Father.*

God, I want to pause within the busyness of the holiday season
to sit before you, read your Word, and wait on you as I recharge
in your presence.

# STOP AND LISTEN

*Martha was distracted with all her preparations; and she came up to Him and said, "Lord, do You not care that my sister has left me to do all the serving alone? Then tell her to help me." But the Lord answered and said to her, "Martha, Martha, you are worried and bothered about so many things; but only one thing is necessary, for Mary has chosen the good part, which shall not be taken away from her."*

LUKE 10:40-42 NASB

The Bible story of Martha and Mary is well known, and many of us feel rather empathetic toward Martha. As women, we manage many responsibilities and tasks, and it requires a lot of hard work and hospitality. This seems especially true as we approach Christmas, when our "to-do" lists grow, and events and celebrations take over our lives.

But sometimes in this season, we worry about the unnecessary things—things that will not last beyond the day. Mary chose the "good part" when Jesus was visiting. She focused on the guest, not the preparations.

*Will you let the Lord show you what things
are distracting you from what really matters?*

As I spend a moment reflecting on you, Jesus, help me to
remember that this is the lasting part of my day. This is where
I gain my strength and hope for all that lies ahead.

# JOURNEY OF HOPE

*"Look, the virgin shall conceive and bear a son,*
*and they shall name him Emmanuel,*
*which means, 'God is with us.'"*

MATTHEW 1:23 NRSV

The day had almost arrived! There were many people waiting for the birth of Jesus. The Jews had long awaited their Messiah, Mary and Joseph were waiting for their firstborn baby, and the Wise Men were looking for the sign. Jesus was the hope that they all looked toward.

There is always a journey involved in waiting for great expectations to be fulfilled. The Jews were preparing themselves for the appointed time, Mary and Joseph had to travel to another town, and the Wise Men had to follow the star. In our own lives, we sometimes forget that the journey is part of the fulfilment of the things that we hope for.

*Are you waiting and hoping for something great to be fulfilled? Take a moment today to reflect on the journey of those who waited expectantly for their Savior.*

God, I pray that hope would remain in my heart for the return of your Son. Help me to look forward to that day with anticipation and joy.

# CARRY THE STORY

*The angel said to them, "Do not be afraid; for see—*
*I am bringing you good news of great joy for all the people:*
*to you is born this day in the city of David a Savior,*
*who is the Messiah, the Lord."*

LUKE 2:9 NRSV

You will probably celebrate Christmas with some manner of tradition. We celebrate with popular cultural traditions and also with our own particular family traditions. Whatever these traditions are, you likely hold them very near to your heart and hope they will last as time goes on.

Have you ever felt lost in all the tradition and wondered if Jesus is truly being celebrated? It's easy to feel disappointed when we forget to elevate Jesus in all of the celebrations. But remember, our celebration of this day actually serves the purpose of carrying the story of Good News forward!

*Take time today to tell the miraculous story
of our Savior's birth, so that it will continue
to be carried through the generations!*

God, instead of frowning on the fact that the world seems to
have commercialized this paramount event in history, help me to
use the festivities to my advantage. Help me to share your story
with others and show them your love.

# HE IS LOVE

*We love because he first loved us. If anyone says,*
*"I love God," and hates his brother, he is a liar;*
*for he who does not love his brother whom he has seen*
*cannot love God whom he has not seen.*

1 JOHN 4:19-20 ESV

God's greatest commandments are to love him and to love one another. Loving him may come easy; after all, he is patient and loving himself. But the second part of his command can be difficult because it means loving intrusive neighbors at the backyard barbecue, offensive cousins at Christmas dinner, rude cashiers at the grocery store check-out, and insufferable guests who have stayed one night too many in the guestroom.

Loving one another is only possible when we love like God loves. When we love out of our humanity, sin gets in the way. Obeying the command to love begins with God's love. When we realize how great his love is for us—how undeserved, unending, and unconditional— we are humbled because we didn't earn it. But he gives it anyway, freely and abundantly, and this spurs us on to love others.

*How can you love others like God loves you?*

Lord, help me represent you to the world. I know it's not easy,
but I want to follow your example and love as you did.
Give me the grace and strength I need to carry this out.

# IT'S A WONDERFUL LIFE

*A man's heart plans his way,*
*But the LORD directs his steps.*

PROVERBS 16:9 NKJV

Have you ever seen the holiday movie *It's a Wonderful Life*? It's an old classic, and it's easy to see why when you watch it. The feelings of the actors onscreen are so pure and raw—and utterly relatable. We have a lot of nights similar to those in the movie: nights where everything goes wrong and we ask, "Why?"

There are so many things in our lives that we simply don't get. We aren't sure why some things happen and other things don't. We have our own lofty dreams and treasured plans, and when they don't work out the way they did in our hearts, we feel lost, angry, and confused.

*Trust in God with all of your heart. Dedicate your plans to him, and allow him to make you his perfect masterpiece.*

God, when everything goes wrong and the plans in my heart don't work out, you know what you're doing. You see what I do not. I might think I have the best plan in the world, but if you are not directing me, my plan will falter.

# THE TABLE

*I bring you good news that will cause great joy for all the*
*people. Today in the town of David a Savior has been born*
*to you; he is the Messiah, the Lord. This will be a sign to you:*
*You will find a baby wrapped in cloths and lying in a manger.*

LUKE 2:10-12 NIV

The Christmas season is like no other. You're invited to Christmas
parties where you get to dress up and make your favorite appetizer.
You can snuggle up on the couch and drink hot chocolate while
watching old classics as your Christmas tree lights twinkle behind
you. You can get together with girlfriends who are in different
stages of life and have a memorable night of laughter and fun.
The season feels almost magical.

One of the best areas to experience this time of year is around the
table. Something beautiful happens when friends and family gather
around delicious food. Conversation can lead almost anywhere.
The beauty of the Christmas season is discovered in smiles,
laughter, and joy-filled memories.

*In this season, is there a time you can gather loved ones together and have a laughter-filled evening?*

Father God, thank you for your provision. Thank you for food, family, friends, and fun. You have blessed me with so much. Help me to create beautiful memories with my family and friends during this season.

# TWINKLING LIGHTS

*"No one lights a lamp and hides it in a clay jar or puts it under a bed. Instead, they put it on a stand, so that those who come in can see the light."*

LUKE 8:16 NIV

Have you ever turned into your neighborhood during this time of year and felt transported to another place entirely? Christmas lights are up, transforming ordinary homes into a magical world of twinkling, beautiful colors. Through the windows of your neighbors' homes you see trees, decorated with ornaments and bulbs. Santa figurines are creatively displayed on rooftops and reindeer are intentionally placed throughout the yard.

If you don't have lights on your own house, enjoy the scene around you. Take time to drive around and reflect on the reason these houses are transformed. The birth of Jesus is a beautiful reminder of the gift of salvation, and this season is a perfect reason to reflect on that in the silence of twinkling lights and illuminated Christmas trees.

*What does this season mean to you amidst
the lights and transformation?*

God, at this time of year my home feels even more
special. More beautiful. More of a blessing. Thank you for
transformation that I see all around me, but I thank you most
for transforming me.

# CHRISTMAS GIFT

*"She will give birth to a son, and you are to give him the name Jesus, because he will save his people from their sins."*

MATTHEW 1:21 NIV

The Christmas season is one of love. It is a season of remembering that the God of the universe came down to earth as a babe, changing everything. It is a season of longing with the adventure of Advent. It is a testament of celebration.

Trees. Twinkling lights. Comfy jammies. Warm tea. Friends. Family. Traditions. Delicious food. Presents. Thoughtfulness. Comfort. Joy. Beauty. Salvation…in the form of a baby.

The Christmas season is one of salvation. It is a beginning to be cherished and devoured at the same time. Recognize the gift of Jesus and what it meant for God to send him down to save us. He truly is the best gift of all.

*In the busyness of this Christmas season, stop and remember what it is all for. You have been saved.*

Thank you, Jesus, for the gift of salvation. There is no greater gift, and there is no way I can repay you for it. I didn't deserve or earn it. You just gave it to me because you love me.

# THE STORYTELLER

*Let the redeemed of the LORD tell their story.*

PSALM 107:2 NIV

Going to the mailbox at this time of year is an exciting adventure. You never know what you're going to get. When you open the mailbox and see all those white envelopes holding Christmas cards, it's thrilling to rip them open, gaze at the pictures, and read the letters. Some families write pages, updating you on every family member and road trip taken. Some friends have a picture with a simple, "Have a very merry Christmas," and others will ride along the middle with a picture and a quick update. Each of these tells a story.

We all have a story to tell: a creative, intricate story designed just for us by the one who determines our steps. It does not matter if your card has a single picture of just you, or you with a husband, or you with a husband and five kids. It does not matter if your card has a picture of your apartment, your dream home, your convertible, or your minivan. It is a story that is beautifully yours and one that should be nourished and nurtured every step of the way.

*Reflect on your current story for a few minutes.*
*What is your prayer as you continue on your journey?*

Father, my story changes as I do. Help me to keep my eyes on
you, the wonderful Storyteller, as change is taking place.

# WHAT DOES GOD SAY?

*Mary responded, "I am the Lord's servant.*
*May everything you have said about me come true."*
*And then the angel left her.*

LUKE 1:38 NLT

In a memorable scene from a movie about teenage girls, a teacher asks a gymnasium full of young women to close their eyes and raise their hands if they've ever said anything bad about another girl. Virtually every hand is raised. The reason this scene rings true is that it is true. And sadly, we are often even harder on ourselves.

In addition to the amazing news that Mary would bear God's son, the angel who visits her in Luke 1 also tells Mary of her goodness, of her favor in God's eyes. Mary was a teenage girl. Chances are, she'd heard—and thought—something less than kind about herself on more than one occasion. Consider her brave, beautiful response with this in mind.

*Are you self-critical? If asked to describe yourself, what would you say? Now think of someone who loves you. What do they say about you? More importantly, what does God have to say about you?*

Father, today I choose to let your words be the truth that I listen to. I join Mary in saying, "May everything you have said about me come true."

# THE ETERNAL GIFT

*"Give glory to God in heaven, and on earth let there be peace among the people who please God."*

LUKE 2:14 NCV

Christmas trees might be secular decorations, but they invoke, in Christians, thoughts of a more precious tree: the cross. Jesus came to us on Christmas day for the purpose of bringing peace to his people through the cross of Calvary.

Christ's mission was to redeem us from every thought, word, or action that didn't match up to our God-likeness. He destroyed our sins and silenced our enemy, permanently, on the cross. He empowered us for victory. Each of us carries his glory as a child of the Most High God. This is a Christmas gift for us to open every day.

*Do you think of the cross as a gift every day?*
*Remember his mercies are new every morning!*

Holy Father, thank you for this gift. Please toss out the broken
ornaments of my life, and remake me according to your glory.
Give me peace. I affirm you as my Lord, and choose to take
orders from you. Thank you for loving me so tenderly.
I love you too.

# GIVING AND SPENDING

*Tell those who are rich not to be proud and not to trust in their money, which will soon be gone, but their pride and trust should be in the living God who always richly gives us all we need for our enjoyment. Tell them to use their money to do good. They should be rich in good works and should give happily to those in need, always being ready to share with others whatever God has given them.*

1 TIMOTHY 6:17-18 TLB

Christmastime is a wonderful time, full of celebration and goodwill. So it seems right to get into the spirit of Christmas and gift-giving. Most of us love the opportunity to shop until late, buy good gifts for our friends and family, and maybe even splurge a little on ourselves.

Generosity is a wonderful thing to exhibit during the Christmas season, but let's not confuse giving with spending. Gifts are wonderful, but as Christmas approaches, allow yourself to dwell on the goodness that you can share with others, particularly those in need.

*Have you fallen into the trap of thinking that spending will give you enjoyment?*

God, you say in your Word that you are the source for my enjoyment. Help me to remember that and to use my money to do good not just to please myself.

# CHRISTMAS TRUCE

*Let the peace of Christ rule in your hearts, since as members
of one body you were called to peace.*

COLOSSIANS 3:15 NIV

In the week leading up to the holiday, soldiers crossed trenches
and ventured into no man's land to exchange seasonal greetings and
food, play football, and take part in joint burial ceremonies and
prisoner swaps. The Christmas truce is seen as a symbolic moment
of peace and humanity amidst one of the most violent events of
human history.

The Christmas spirit is often talked of throughout this season, and
while at times it seems to take away from the pure celebration of
Christ, it is encouraging to read of stories where goodwill seems to
conquer in the midst of a stressful and often hurtful world.

*Is there a time and place this Christmas for you to offer
a Christmas truce? Can you set aside family differences,
long-standing arguments, or even regrets,
in order to create harmony?*

Father, help me to be intentional this year about being gracious
to my family. I want you to be evident in my life especially to
those in my family who need you so much.

# JOURNEY OF
# THE WISE MEN

*When they saw the star, they were filled with joy! They entered the house and saw the child with his mother, Mary, and they bowed down and worshiped him. Then they opened their treasure chests and gave him gifts of gold, frankincense, and myrrh.*

MATTHEW 2:10-11 NLT

In the Bible, the wise men traveled a great distance to find the Savior. They were armed with gifts, and when they found him, they presented those gifts in honor of him. Can you even imagine what that must have been like? Knowing you were staring at the Savior of the world as a tiny baby, and trying to digest what his presence would mean to the world? It's incredible.

This time of year, what can we do to honor him? How can we be his hands in helping others? The Christmas season is a great time to engage in something unique because there are usually a lot of great opportunities. How can you spread his love in a different way?

*How could you spread the love of Jesus this Christmas season? Is there something you've been wanting to do but haven't yet? This might be the perfect opportunity.*

God, give me wisdom this season to find a way to spread your love that is effective and unique! I am excited to share your goodness with others.

# BOXING DAY

*All who are under the yoke of slavery should consider their masters worthy of full respect, so that God's name and our teaching may not be slandered.*

1 TIMOTHY 6:1 NIV

In many countries around the world, the day after Christmas is called Boxing Day: a tradition that began in a time when tradespeople were given Christmas boxes of money or presents to acknowledge good service throughout the year.

While we don't like to think of ourselves as servants these days, many of us are involved in employment or some type of service. The Bible says much about those that have shown diligence and respect to those who are in authority.

There is a higher purpose to us respecting our employers. We may not get our Boxing Day reward for recognition of our service, but we will be honoring God's name as a witness of Christian living.

Be encouraged as you go to your place of work (whether home, study, or employment), knowing that as you show good service, you are positively representing the name of Jesus.

Father, I want to be acknowledged as a good and faithful servant by you one day. Help me to represent you well in my workplace.

# THE SELF ELF

*Do nothing from selfish ambition or conceit, but in humility regard others as better than yourselves. Let each of you look not to your own interests, but to the interests of others.*

PHILIPPIANS 2:3-4 NRSV

Can we ever truly grasp what Jesus had to give up in order to become human and walk this earth with us? Scripture tells us that although Jesus had equality with God, he gave up his supreme entitlement to become human. We may never quite understand this act, but I think we can accept that Jesus' birth and death on the cross was our ultimate example of sacrifice.

We may be involved in the spirit of giving this season, but are we involved in the spirit of giving up? Are we willing to sacrifice, as in the example of Jesus, regarding others before ourselves? This is not to attribute a higher worth based on superior authority or qualities, but to understand people's value in light of Christ.

*Do you recognize selfish ambition in your life?*

Jesus, right now I choose to reflect on your sacrifice. In thankfulness, I commit to imitate you by seeing the good in others and pursuing their interests above my own.

# WHEN YOU FEEL STUCK

*The Sovereign Lord is my strength! He makes me as surefooted as a deer, able to tread upon the heights.*

HABAKKUK 3:19 NLT

"Local authorities are reporting blizzard conditions on the Interstate…" Did your pulse just quicken, your muscles tense? No one likes to feel stuck, and blinding snow and unmoving vehicles on every side can cause even the most rational, laid-back woman to imagine leaping from her car and running over rooftops and across hoods, action hero style. What a fun way to test out the traction on your new winter boots. Or not. Anyway, stuck is stuck, right?

Maybe we feel stuck in our everyday lives. A job that doesn't utilize our gifts, a relationship that's more take than give, a habit that's edging toward addiction. Unlike that snow-covered freeway-turned-parking-lot, there is a direction to turn when circumstances have you feeling boxed in. Turn your face toward the Lord; let him fill you with the strength to move.

*Where are you stuck right now? Professionally, personally, or perhaps in your prayer life, is there an area where you've simply stopped moving?*

God I need your surefooted strength today. Help me to follow where you lead me. I want to be obedient to your call.

# THE FATHER'S LOVE

*"If a man has a hundred sheep but one of the sheep gets lost, he will leave the other ninety-nine on the hill and go to look for the lost sheep. I tell you the truth, if he finds it he is happier about that one sheep than about the ninety-nine that were never lost."*

MATTHEW 18:12-13 NCV

Regardless of how beautifully or how imperfectly your earthly father showed his love, your heavenly Father's love is utterly boundless. Rest in that thought a moment. There is nothing you can do to change how he feels about you. Nothing.

We spend so much time trying to make ourselves more lovable, from beauty regimens to gourmet baking, to being there for pretty much everyone. It's easy to forget we are already perfectly loved. Our Father loves us more than we can imagine. And he would do anything for us. Anything.

Who do you love most fiercely, most protectively, most
desperately here on earth? What would you do for them?
Know that it's a mere fraction, nearly immeasurable,
of what God would do for you.

God, I thank you for your complete and astounding love for me.
You come search me out when I am lost and you rejoice when
you find me. Thank you for watching over me.

# NO WORDS

*Then they sat on the ground with him for seven days and nights. No one said a word to Job, for they saw that his suffering was too great for words.*

Sometimes, all you need to do to be a hero is show up. We love to talk, don't we? Words of encouragement, words of comfort, words of advice. Even if you are the quiet type, you know a woman who is rarely at a loss for words.

But occasionally, there really are no words. Someone you love is hurting, and you truly don't know what to say. Your presence says it all. In those moments you feel lost for words, if God occupies the central place in your heart, he'll make your heart known.

*How easy or difficult would it be for you to simply be with someone in their sorrow and not try to "fix" them? Do you know someone who would be blessed today by the silent, loving presence of someone who loves them?*

God, show me how to be silent and comforting to someone who needs that. Help me to speak only words that you provide. I want to be a good friend to those you have placed in my life.

# THE REAL THING

*When they arrived, Samuel took one look at Eliab and thought, "Surely this is the LORD's anointed!" But the LORD said to Samuel, "Don't judge by his appearance or height, for I have rejected him. The LORD doesn't see things the way you see them. People judge by outward appearance, but the LORD looks at the heart."*

1 SAMUEL 16:6-7 NLT

*Is that real?* Whether jewelry, hair color, purse, or body part, there's real, and there's imitation. Neither choice is inherently wrong or right. Why we choose as we do—and where we compromise— reveals our hearts. And it's our hearts that matter to God.

Make no mistake, a sister who shuns makeup and hasn't painted her house trim in years can be every bit as guilty of vanity and pride as one who won't leave her own bedroom until she appears flawless and has an eight-person grounds crew.

*Spend some time examining your heart with God today.*

God, you don't care how much I spend on shoes, how much time I spend in front of the mirror, or how fabulous my home is. But you do care about why those things matter—or don't—to me. Help me to want the right things for the right reasons.

# FORGIVENESS

*"When you stand praying, if you hold anything against anyone, forgive them, so that your Father in heaven may forgive you your sins."*

MARK 11:25 NIV

It seems like most families and many circles of friends contain at least two people who aren't speaking to one another—and haven't for years. Perhaps you know someone. Perhaps you are the someone. Occasionally, the offense itself is truly unforgivable: abuse, betrayal, or complete disregard. Other times, and considerably more often, even the people involved admit the silliness of the quarrel and are no longer angry about it. But they're still not speaking with the person.

What do we gain when we hold onto bitterness? Bitterness. When we refuse to let go of anger, what do we find in our clenched fists? Anger. While an offense may be unforgivable, no person is. Jesus proved that when he died for all of us. And here's a fact often overlooked, especially by those of us who seem to like our little balls of anger: God withholds our forgiveness until we have forgiven others. Ouch.

*Believe what Scripture tells you.*
*Open your hand and surrender your grudges.*
*Ask the Father to refill you with peace.*

God, I am in need of your forgiveness daily. Help me to extend forgiveness to others so I can walk in right relationship with you.

# FLIP THE SWITCH

*The way of the good person is like the light of dawn,*
*growing brighter and brighter until full daylight.*
*But the wicked walk around in the dark;*
*they can't even see what makes them stumble.*

PROVERBS 4:18-19 NCV

Have you ever walked through your home at night, thinking that you could make it without turning a light on, only to stumble on something unexpectedly set in your path? When you cannot see where you are going, you are likely to get tripped up. On the other hand, your way is obvious when you simply turn on a light.

The Bible tells us that walking in righteousness is just like walking in the bright light of day. But choosing rebellion is like stumbling around in a deep darkness. You never know what hit you until it's already too late.

*Are you choosing the light? Is your path brightly lit? Or are*
*you standing in total darkness? If so, then flip the switch!*
*Pray that you will make wise choices.*

God, I seek your wisdom for my life. You shine brightly for
me. I let you in today and ask that you will be my eternal light,
illuminating my days.

# LOSING TO GAIN

*"If you try to hang on to your life, you will lose it. But if you give up your life for my sake, you will save it."*

MATTHEW 16:25 NLT

The key to growing in your faith is simple. There must be less of us in order to have more of God. To allow more of his presence into our lives, we must give up more of ourselves. We need to place our lives before him as an offering and give him our all.

The world would say that giving up ourselves is a loss. We've been taught for years that we must put ourselves first. Our fellow man would say that we need to make ourselves a priority. But oh, are they missing out! When we give ourselves over completely to God, we get to share in his glory and in his great joy. Setting aside our earthly pleasures for heavenly treasures means we gain a lot more than what this world could ever offer us.

*Empty yourself of the desires of your flesh and allow God to fill you with his presence.*

God, as I empty myself of selfish desires, I won't feel a lack. Thank you that it will cause me to overflow with life and light, spilling out everywhere for others to see. I know that I need to become less so I can gain more of you.

# IN SUNSHINE AND STORM

*When times are good, be happy;*
*but when times are bad, consider this:*
*God has made the one as well as the other.*
*Therefore, no one can discover*
*anything about their future.*

ECCLESIASTES 7:14 NIV

It's easy to feel happy on a sunny day, when all is well, the birds are singing, and life is going along swimmingly. But what happens when waters are rougher, bad news comes, or the days feel just plain hard?

God wants us to feel gladness when times are good. He has made each and every day. We are called to rejoice in all of them whether good or bad. Happiness is determined by our circumstances, but true joy comes when we can find the silver linings, hidden in our darkest hours—when we can sing his praises no matter what. We don't know what the future holds for us here on earth, but we can find our delight in the knowledge that our eternity is set in beauty.

*Is your happiness determined by your circumstance?*
*Pray that you will discover true joy in your Creator.*

God, give me a deep and abiding satisfaction in each day that
goes beyond my human understanding. Help me to see the
beauty in the future you have for me.

# IN THIS TOGETHER

*Christ's love compels us, because we are convinced that one died for all, and therefore all died. And he died for all, that those who live should no longer live for themselves but for him who died for them and was raised again.*

2 CORINTHIANS 5:14-15 NIV

We can often find ourselves seeing all the ways in which we are different. You take your coffee black, and your friend takes hers with more cream than caffeine. You vote one way, your neighbor votes another. Maggie is an introvert, and Melanie won't stop talking.

But here's the thing we have in common: no matter who we are or what we believe, Jesus Christ died for us all. Each and every one of us falls into the category of "all." There's nobody left out. He died for Maggie, he died for Melanie, and he died for your neighbor who votes differently than you do. One man died for everyone, and this puts us all on the same page.

*Look for the similarities between you and those around you.*
*We are all in this together!*

God, I pray today that you will help me break down walls in my
relationships with others and help me to stand on the truth.
I want to communicate your love to everyone.

# BOLD AND CONFIDENT

*My voice You shall hear in the morning, O LORD;*
*In the morning I will direct it to You,*
*And I will look up.*

PSALM 5:3 NKJV

Each and every day, we are given the most incredible opportunity. We are given the chance to talk to a God who has been in our shoes. A man who literally walked the walk. He is waiting for us to walk up to him and ask him anything.

Jesus went through the same things we do during his time on earth, so he truly understands where we're coming from when we approach him. We don't need to muster up our courage! He wants us to be confident. Esther was bold when she approached her king about saving her people, and that guy was known to make rash and terrible decisions! We get to talk to a King who is known for his mercy.

*Are you holding back tentatively in your time with your heavenly King? Be bold, and be confident!*

Father, thank you that you love me. You understand me. You want what's best for me. I am so grateful that you show me grace and mercy wherever and whenever I seek it from you.

# DANCE UNHINDERED

*"It was before the LORD, who chose me rather than your father or anyone from his house when he appointed me ruler over the LORD's people Israel—I will celebrate before the LORD. I will become even more undignified than this, and I will be humiliated in my own eyes. But by these slave girls you spoke of, I will be held in honor."*

2 SAMUEL 6:21-22 NIV

Peer pressure is real, even for adults. We often worry about how we will look in the eyes of others. *Do I look okay today?* we wonder. *I forgot to bring the garbage can in. What will the neighbors think?* we ask ourselves.

There was at least one person who didn't care what others thought of him. King David was so excited after winning a big battle that he went whooping and dancing, praising God as he marched home to his family. When his wife scorned him for looking foolish, he had no time for her words.

*Are you worried about what others think,*
*or are you concerned with what God thinks of you?*

God, today I dance in your presence. I don't care what it looks like! I want to celebrate life with you and I know you delight in rejoicing with me too.

# EYE ON YOU

*In him we were also chosen, having been predestined according to the plan of him who works out everything in conformity with the purpose of his will, in order that we, who were the first to put our hope in Christ, might be for the praise of his glory.*

EPHESIANS 1:11-12 NIV

Did you know that long before you decided to take the plunge and accept Christ into your heart as your Savior, he had his eye on you? He was waiting for you to come to him so that he could share with you his eternal gift. God wanted glorious living for you. And oh, how he celebrated when you made that decision!

It is through Christ that we discover who we are. When we put our hope in him, we find ourselves. It's in him that we learn what we are living for. And he works all of our lives together as Christians for the greater good.

*You were chosen by God. He waited for you, and he rejoiced when you came to him. Celebrate with him today!*

I praise you, God, for the gift you have given me in eternal salvation. You are so good!

# DOING THE RIGHT THING

*The love of God is this, that we obey his commandments.*
*And his commandments are not burdensome.*

1 JOHN 5:3 NRSV

When we buy into the lie that how we live our earthly lives determines whether or not we will have eternal life, we lose sight of the entire point of the Gospel. Legalism says that doing good works will make you right with God. But the people in the Bible who dedicated their lives to "doing the right thing" (the Pharisees) are the very same people who put Jesus on the cross.

Legalism isn't a holier form of God-worship; it's self-worship. When we give ourselves a role in our own salvation, we are claiming to be able to do something only Jesus is capable of. The grace of Christ alone is what saves us.

*Your obedience doesn't carry the weight of your righteousness. You have righteousness through faith in the Son of God. You have only to love him.*

God, I desire to obey you because I know that obedience will bring me closer to you. I love you and I want to be close to you.

# PERSEVERANCE

*Do not throw away this confident trust in the Lord.
Remember the great reward it brings you! Patient endurance
is what you need now, so that you will continue to do God's
will. Then you will receive all that he has promised.*

HEBREWS 10:35-36 NLT

Do you remember when you first decided to follow Christ?
Maybe you felt like a huge weight was being lifted off you, or that
the peace and joy you'd been searching for was finally yours. You
were filled with excitement in your newfound life, and you felt
ready to take on the world in the name of Jesus.

Following God may come easy at first. We accept him into our lives
and are swept into his love with incredible hope. But as time goes
on, old temptations return, and threaten to shake our resolve. The
confidence we felt in our relationship at first lessens as we wonder
if we have what it takes to stick it out in this Christian life.

*Perhaps you have lost the confidence you had at first.
Or maybe you are still in that place of complete confidence
and trust. Either way, step boldly forward into all
that God has for you.*

God, I want to remain confident in you. I know you will
accomplish what you have promised. When following you gets
hard, help me to press in even harder and remember that I will
be richly rewarded for my perseverance.

# PERFECT LOVE

*We know the love that God has for us, and we trust that love.
God is love. Those who live in love live in God, and God
lives in them. This is how love is made perfect in us: that we
can be without fear on the day God judges us, because in this
world we are like him.*

1 JOHN 4:16-17 NCV

Does anyone know the *real* you? The you that hasn't been edited
or exaggerated?

Putting up a false front in our relationships is a direct expression
of our own fear. When we are afraid to be truly known, we lose
out on the most incredible gift that can be given in relationship—
honest love. We sacrifice genuine relationship on the altar of our
own insecurity and fear.

Lay down your need to be perceived as perfect, and allow yourself
to be loved for who you truly are.

*Are you afraid to be fully known?*

God, wash my fear away with your perfect love.
I want to truly understand that you love me for who I am.
I don't need to pretend to be anything I'm not with you.

# SANCTUARY

*"Let them make Me a sanctuary,
that I may dwell among them."*

EXODUS 25:8 NKJV

Since sin entered the world in the Garden of Eden there has been a divide between the holy God and humanity. But throughout history, God has created ways for us to still have fellowship with him despite the separation that sin caused.

God wants to be with us. He didn't shrug his shoulders when sin entered the world and reconcile himself to the fact that he wouldn't be able to have a close relationship with us any longer. No, rather, he went to the greatest lengths to still be with us because his love for us is that intense.

God wants to dwell among us. Not just visit. Not just talk sometimes. He wants his presence to be constantly among us.

*Are you creating a sanctuary in your life
where God can dwell?*

God, I want to foster an atmosphere that welcomes you.
I know you long to be near me and that was made possible
when you sent your Son to die for my sin.

# MONEY TROUBLE

*Keep your lives free from the love of money,*
*and be content with what you have; for he has said,*
*"I will never leave you or forsake you."*

HEBREWS 13:5 NRSV

Sometimes money can feel like water in our hands. It slips right through our fingers, and is gone as soon as it's acquired.

As Christians, we know that we should trust God with our every need. But do we really? Are we confident that no matter what circumstances come our way, God is going to take care of our finances? Or do we become consumed with worry that we will not have enough?

Right after God tells us not to love money, he reminds us that he'll never leave or forsake us. He knew that we would worry about our finances. He knew that fear would come far more easily than contentment.

*Remember that no matter how little or how much money
you have, God is in control.*

Father, you are more than able to provide for all my needs, and
you will never forsake me. Thank you that I can rely on you when
I have trouble with my finances.

# THIRST FOR PURE WATER

*I want more than anything*
*to be in the courtyards of the LORD's Temple.*
*My whole being wants*
*to be with the living God.*

PSALM 84:2 NCV

Have you ever noticed that the more consistently you drink water, the more your body thirsts for it? And the less you drink water, the less you consciously desire it. Though you still need water to live, you become satisfied with small amounts of it disguised in other foods and drinks. But for a body that has become accustomed to pure water on a daily basis, only straight water will quench its thirst.

The same principle applies to God's presence in our lives. The more we enter his presence, the more we long to stay there. The more we sit at his feet and listen to what he has to say, the more we need his Word to continue living. But if we allow ourselves to become satisfied with candy-coated truth and second hand revelation, we will slowly begin to lose our hunger for the pure, untainted presence of the living God.

*Does your entire being long to be with God? Press into Jesus until you no longer can be satisfied with anything less than the purest form of his presence.*

Cultivate my hunger and fascination with you, God, until I literally crave you. I want to spend my life feasting on your truth, knowing your character, and adoring your heart.

# PERFECTION

*His divine power has granted to us everything pertaining to life and godliness, through the true knowledge of Him who called us by His own glory and excellence.*

2 PETER 1:3 NASB

Each of us is keenly aware of our own weaknesses. We know all our flaws too well and we make eliminating them our goal. But no matter how much effort we put out, we can never and will never achieve perfection.

Despite most of us realizing that we will never be perfect, we still put unreasonable pressure on ourselves. Whether in a task, in our character, or in our walk with Christ, we easily become frustrated when we reach for perfection and can't grasp. But if we allow perfectionism to drive our performance, then we will quench our own potential and inhibit our effectiveness.

*When you mess up, God has to take over and the result of that action is always perfection.*

God, thank you for the freedom to not be perfect. Your power is all the more perfect when displayed in my weakness. When I am not the main point, you are. That's the way it should be.

# STILLNESS

*Be still, and know that I am God;*
*I will be exalted among the nations,*
*I will be exalted in the earth!*

PSALM 46:10 NKJV

Dusk settles on a chilly winter night. A gray fog hovers and snow begins to fall: cold, blustering snow…the kind that sticks. The snow keeps coming until you can barely see one hundred feet in front of you. In the woods it's quiet; all you can hear is the gentle wind, and all you can see is snow and trees. A pure white blanket of snow restores the earth, and as it falls, it restores you.

Sometimes we have to get outside of the noise and chaos of our own four walls. We have to step out into the snow, or the sun, or the breeze. We have to get alone, get silent, and clear the clutter from our minds and hearts as we stand in God's natural sanctuary.

There is so much power in the stillness of knowing God as you stand serene in the world he created.

*The busyness of your life will always be there, but never forget to take the moments you can to stop and know your God.*

In these precious moments I spend with you, God, I find refreshment and strength to take on whatever will come next.

# OUR FATHER IN HEAVEN

*The eyes of the LORD watch over those who do right;*
*his ears are open to their cries for help.*

PSALM 34:15 NLT

Do we know in the depths of our hearts that our prayers are heard: both the shouting cries for help and the gentle whispers of thanksgiving? He knows our every thought before we even think it. This is the Father that created us and calls us by name. We are his beloved daughters.

Believe it, beautiful women. We need to let the truth sink into the very deepest parts of our hearts and rest there in thanksgiving. His Word is truth, and he tells us time and time again that he will answer our prayer because we trust in him (see 1 Chronicles 5:20). Whether through song, action, thought, or speech, he delights in hearing our prayers.

*Do you take time daily to pray to your loving Father?*
*If not, start the practice of talking with him in the car,*
*in the shower, or sitting in silence in your room.*

Thank you, God, that what I say to you doesn't have to be fancy or long. You desire my honest conversation and communion with you more than a thousand pretty words.

# LESS OF THE WORLD

*I will tell of the kindnesses of the LORD,*
*the deeds for which he is to be praised,*
*according to all the LORD has done for us…*
*according to his compassion and many kindnesses.*

ISAIAH 63:7 NIV

Jesus died on the cross to set us free. He suffered, he wept, he bled, he endured. Forever. For our freedom. What are we doing with that freedom? Are we continually playing it safe? Are we doing all we can to cast aside our fleshly desires and focus on the one great prize? How do we spend our time and energy?

Let's pray that we desire less of the world and more of Christ. Let's pray that we see our freedom for what it is. Let's pray for worldly desires to dissipate and hearts that cultivate courage to stand for what is good and right.

*How can you stop focusing on stuff and instead focus on furthering his kingdom?*

Father, it's not an easy task to lay aside my selfish desires. The world tells me to do what makes me happy. Help me to desire less of the world's idea of wealth and more of your eternal riches.

# BALANCE BEAM

*"Seek first the kingdom of God and his righteousness,*
*and all these things will be added to you."*

MATTHEW 6:33 ESV

Have you ever taken an exercise or dance class where balance is a crucial component? Or gone for a run and knew that finding a comfortable pace was the only way you were going to complete the run?

Women have a lot of responsibility. Whatever season of life we are in, we most likely wear a hat that fits somewhere into the category of entrepreneur, scheduler, baker, driver, chef, employee, sister, daughter, friend, wife, or mother. You might wear only one hat, but most likely, you're juggling multiple hats a day. This can be a blessing, but it can also feel like a weight. Finding balance amidst the busyness of life is crucial to your hat fitting comfortably.

What can you change about your day today to give you more balance? Think about a meeting you could shorten so you can take a quick walk, or inviting a friend to lunch, or skipping the gym and going to a coffee shop for an hour to read.

God, with the many hats I try on, I want to make sure I find the right ones to wear at the right times. I want the balance of life that makes me a better me. I need your wisdom to figure out where that balance is.

# MYSTERY AND HOPE

*Since through God's mercy we have this ministry, we do not lose heart. Rather, we have renounced secret and shameful ways; we do not use deception, nor do we distort the word of God. On the contrary, by setting forth the truth plainly we commend ourselves to everyone's conscience in the sight of God…For God, who said, "Let light shine out of darkness," made his light shine in our hearts to give us the light of the knowledge of God's glory displayed in the face of Christ.*

2 Corinthians 4:1-2, 6 niv

There is so much mystery to life. So many unanswered questions and unknowns. Faith in and of itself is mysterious. In order to live a faith-filled life, we accept the elements of mystery because we know what goes hand-in-hand with it…hope. Hope is God telling us that his purpose is bigger than any unknown. When we walk through anything, no matter how great a mystery, God is walking alongside us.

God doesn't promise us an explanation, and therein lies the mystery. But he does promise his presence, and that is an unfailing truth. When we walk through deep waters, he is there.

*Have you had a moment of mystery?*
*An unexplained circumstance or situation*
*that you wish you could ask God about?*

Father, I know deep in my heart that hope is waiting
on the other end of the mystery.

# AFTER THE HEART

*You have not received a spirit of slavery leading to fear*
*again, but you have received a spirit of adoption as sons*
*by which we cry out, "Abba! Father!"*

ROMANS 8:15 NASB

There is a difference in maturity of faith when we start to see God as our Father instead of just our Creator. We start to discern his voice amidst all the other voices, and we recognize that our actions, thoughts, and lack of trust can leave him yearning for us to be back in his grasp.

As much as we might feel there are other people God desires more or is more proud of because of their spiritual maturity, it is a lie. Sweet daughters of the one true King, he pursues our hearts. He desires our love. He yearns for the times we speak to him.

*Do you know that God pursues you? Let that thought permeate your being. He—the Creator of the universe, Abba Father, Alpha and Omega, I AM—pursues you!*

God, you long for me to know you. I am encouraged that no matter where I am on my spiritual walk, you will not stop pursuing me.

# REJOICE TODAY

*This is the day the LORD has made;*
*We will rejoice and be glad in it.*

PSALM 118:24 NKJV

Winter is fully upon us, and even if you live somewhere that isn't blanketed in cold and snow, it's still winter. It's not as warm outside, and there's not as much life in nature. If you do live where winter is cold, you may be growing tired of boots, hats, scarves (well, maybe not scarves), and puffy, shapeless coats. Looking outside, there may not be much to feel particularly joyful about.

Yet, we are called to rejoice—today. There are days we see his handiwork everywhere we look, and there are days that just seem to happen. Be certain; the Creator has created, and this day is it.

*Look harder, closer, at today. Find a patch of blue sky, recall a night of sledding, light a fire. Turn your heart toward God, and rejoice and be glad for today.*

Father God, today is an offering from you to me.
That in itself is cause for celebration! Thank you for life and love.
I rejoice in you today.

# THE GOOD FIGHT

*I remind you to fan into flame the gift of God, which is in you…for the Spirit God gave us does not make us timid, but gives us power, love and self-discipline…join with me in suffering for the gospel, by the power of God.*

2 TIMOTHY 1:6-8 NIV

In order to feel confident in what that looks like, we need to understand that having courage is God-given. Having courage to fight for our brothers and sisters is given through the Spirit of God. The same Spirit that lives in him is alive in us—that thought alone must push us.

Second Timothy promises us that our spirit gives us power, love, and self-discipline. In order to see the fullness of God's Spirit, we need to take a step. It doesn't need to be a full-blown jump—just a single step to ignite a flame. A step might be taking a colleague to coffee, asking your waiter if they belong to a church, or reaching out to that neighbor you've always wondered about.

*What does stepping out and joining the fight look like for you?*

God, I know a step is powerful; it can plant a seed the size of a mustard seed. That same mustard seed can move a mountain, further your kingdom, and glorify your name. Show me what my next step is.

# GEMS

*The heartfelt counsel of a friend*
*is as sweet as perfume and incense.*

PROVERBS 27:9 NLT

When you sign up for a competitive team sport, you have a basic understanding that you're going to have to work hard and that emotions will run high to win and succeed. You know that you'll win some, you'll lose some, and that somewhere along the way you'll start to feel good about playing the game whether you win or lose.

Playing a competitive team sport can sometimes feel the same as building relationships with other women. We win some—forming incredible relationships—and others we lose. We were created uniquely, and while we are asked to love one another, it doesn't mean that we hope for a best-friend relationship with each woman we meet.

When we do find those friends, those precious few who make us better people by encouraging us and making us laugh, we need to hold on tight and enjoy the rare gems they are.

*Do you have a friend that holds you accountable but also lifts you up when you need it? Share how much that friend means to you today.*

God, I thank you for friends that hold me accountable. I ask that you would continue to bring people into my life that challenge me and encourage me in my walk with you.

# HERO

*Grace to you and peace from God our Father and the Lord Jesus Christ, who gave Himself for our sins so that He might rescue us from this present evil age, according to the will of our God and Father, to whom be the glory forevermore.*

GALATIANS 1:3-5 NIV

He came down, in love, and rescued us. He delivered us from our sin.

We are forever his. And we are forever freed. There is no other love that loves without borders. And it is free. Let that resonate in your heart. He came down in love and rescued you...for free.

Jesus truly is the hero in our fairy tale. No matter what we experience today, we should let that sink in.

*Have you ever doubted God's love for you? Reread this devotion and let the truth of it sink deep into your heart.*

Jesus, you have rescued me. Thank you for your love that is without boundary.

# LOVE WELL

*Follow God's example, therefore, as dearly loved children and walk in the way of love, just as Christ loved us and gave himself up for us as a fragrant offering and sacrifice to God.*

EPHESIANS 5:1-2 NIV

If we do anything right, let it be that we love well. Loving well looks different for each person, but we know it when we do it: when we love whole-heartedly. We can't change the entire world—only Jesus can do that—but we can change the world for one person.

There are big things you can do to love well, but loving well can be done in little, everyday moments too. We love despite feelings. We love when it's tough. We love when we don't necessarily want to. We love well because we are called to: because God loved us first.

*In what ways can you love well? Are there some you don't feel you love well in where you can aim higher?*

God, help me love the way you do.
Please give me your heart for those you have placed in my life.
I cannot love in my own strength.

# THE CALL FOR HELP

*I look up to the hills,*
*but where does my help come from?*
*My help comes from the LORD,*
*who made heaven and earth*

PSALM 121:1-2 NCV

Depending on the type of person you are, you may not be very good at asking for help. There are those who like to be the helpers: they do best serving others because they feel capable and useful. Then there are those who gladly accept service any time they are given the opportunity. Neither is better than the other, and both have their positive elements.

In different seasons of life, natural helpers may need to be the ones receiving help. Sometimes this is hard to accept, and we have to be careful not to let pride take control. Asking for help is part of being vulnerable: we push everything aside to say, "I can't do this alone." God has put people in our lives who love to help, but they won't know we need it until we ask.

*Can you easily ask for help? God asks you to take a chance
on the people he's intricately placed in your life.*

Thank you, God, for the people you have placed in my life for
me to lean on. I am amazed by how much stronger I feel when I
have someone to help me carry the load. I want to be that person
for others as well.

# CHEER FOR THE PRIZE

*May the God who gives endurance and encouragement*
*give you the same attitude of mind toward each other*
*that Christ Jesus had.*

ROMANS 15:5 NIV

Have you ever watched cheerleaders at a sporting event? Smiling, bubbly, energetic, yelling for their beloved team. What we don't see is what might be going on underneath all of that encouragement. Everyone has their issues. And yet there they are, faithfully devoted to their team because they know the prize at the end.

In this same way, let us encourage one another in our faith. Imagine our Abba Father's joy when he sees us lifting each other up in praise and loving despite whatever we might have going on. There is so much to be gained in relationship with other believers whether on the receiving or giving end. And the prize at the end is eternity. There is nothing greater.

*What are some ways you can encourage others?*

G od, I know you delight in seeing me give of my time and talents. You have blessed me with talents for the specific purpose of sharing with others. Help me not to be selfish with my gifts.

# CLAY

*Now, O Lᴏʀᴅ, you are our Father;*
*we are the clay, and you are our potter;*
*we are all the work of your hand.*

Iꜱᴀɪᴀʜ 64:8 ᴇꜱᴠ

Life can be busy. Whatever season you are in, there are always things to be done. More often times than not, our wellbeing is cast aside because of all the other things that need to be tended to. Our Creator says that we are jars of clay. If left out and not tended to, that jar of clay can dry out and crack.

If we can give God our obedience and our time, he promises us his abundance and peace, quenching our very driest parts. Oh, daughters, the renewal we receive when we sit in his presence, letting him fill our spirit with his love and gentle, encouraging words!

*When do you feel most renewed? Take time today to be refreshed by his Word and sit with him in prayer.*

God, you hear my cries for renewal wherever I am. You hear my whispers of longing for your peace to fill my soul. Come be with me now I ask.

# LET GOD WIN

*Truthful words stand the test of time,*
*but lies are soon exposed.*

PROVERBS 12:19 NLT

Don't believe the lies. There is an enemy out there who wants to steal, kill, and destroy. One of the most powerful ways he does that is through filling our hearts with things we think are true about ourselves. Those lies fill our minds with hatred, so that when we look in the mirror, we start hating what we see. *I'm so ugly. I don't deserve anything good in my life. I screwed up again; why do I even try?*

Beloved, God loves us! He knits us together and sets us apart. He cherishes every breath we take, and in the name of Jesus, we can rebuke the enemy so those lies no longer fill our heads and overtake our hearts.

*What are the lies that tear you down?*

Jesus, lift the veil from my eyes so I can see clearly. The truth is that I serve a God who would move mountains for me, a Father who loves me more than anything, and a Creator who delights in seeing me smile.

# CYCLE

*To the praise of the glory of His grace, which He freely bestowed on us in the Beloved. In Him we have redemption through His blood, the forgiveness of our trespasses, according to the riches of His grace which He lavished on us.*

EPHESIANS 1:6-8 NASB

Have you ever said or done something that you immediately regretted? It just happened: that horrible moment that we replay over and over again. Then, maybe a few days later, something similar happens. Why does this happen? Why can't we exercise more self-control?

Those moments are the vicious cycle of our humanness. Thankfully, through the blood of Jesus Christ and our repentance, we are forgiven, set free, and released of the burden of our mistakes. We are given a clean slate to start over. And some days that gift feels bigger than others. Some days we rely heavily on the grace of our Lord and Savior just to get through the day. And that is okay.

*Have you had a "moment" recently? Do you know you are
forgiven through the blood of Jesus?*

God, I accept your gift; I am forgiven. Help me to forgive myself
and keep moving forward.

# HIGHWAYS

*"My thoughts are not your thoughts,*
*nor are your ways my ways, says the Lord.*
*For as the heavens are higher than the earth,*
*so are my ways higher than your ways*
*and my thoughts than your thoughts."*

ISAIAH 55:8-9 NRSV

If you stop to think about it, most of our conversations are made up of a dialogue of various opinions. We talk about the facts, for sure, but the meaningful stuff comes when we start to influence those facts with our own sentiments.

There's nothing wrong with searching for meaning in situations and trying to make sense of the complexities of life. It's possible that the quest for understanding is an integral part of our human nature. However, we ultimately need to surrender our understanding and opinions to God's truth.

In the context of this scripture, God is speaking specifically about his mercy for his people.

*Are there certain "ways of God" that you just can't make sense of in your life? Be encouraged to surrender your thoughts in order to trust his.*

God, I admit there are ways of yours that I simply cannot understand. I know I need to trust your Word that says your ways and thoughts are higher than mine. Help me not to be offended by your ways.

# NEW EVERY MORNING

*Because of the LORD's great love, we are not consumed,*
*for his compassions never fail.*
*They are new every morning;*
*great is your faithfulness.*

LAMENTATIONS 3:22-23 NIV

Some days it is good to reflect on exactly what God has saved us from. As a nation, Israel knew what it was to fail God time and time again. They rebelled against him and they deserved punishment; yet, God chose to redeem them, over and over again. His love for his people compelled him to show mercy.

We are not unlike the Israelites in our rebellion and turning away from God's purposes. We are also not unlike the Israelites in that God has incredible compassion for us. In sending his Son, Jesus Christ, God proved once and for all that his compassion will never fail.

Why does God's compassion have to appear new every morning? Because we can barely go a day without failing. We need to be reminded of God's faithfulness so that we can turn toward him, daily.

*Did you fail God yesterday, or today? His mercy endures!*

Thank you, Father, for your compassion every single morning.
I confess my sin and I am ready to start the day new.

# DON'T BE ASHAMED

*I am suffering now because I tell the Good News, but I am not ashamed, because I know Jesus, the One in whom I have believed. And I am sure he is able to protect what he has trusted me with until that day.*

2 TIMOTHY 1:12 NCV

Have you ever tried to wade upstream through a river, or swim against a strong current? It is hard! Sometimes this is how we can feel as a Christian in a world full of unbelievers. Our modern culture is full of political correctness and accepting all beliefs, but when it comes to Christianity, it can feel like anything we say is offensive!

Paul was put in prison a number of times for offending the people of his time. He seemed to suffer gladly because he was convinced that Jesus was the Savior and that his mission was to share this good news with the world. Paul was convinced of the truth, and because of this, he was not ashamed!

Do you tend to keep quiet about your faith in Jesus? Are you worried about suffering, or being mocked for your beliefs? Take time each day to develop your relationship with him.

Jesus, the more I know you, the more confident I will be in what I believe. Help me to imitate Paul's dedication to sharing the gospel and trust you to protect me.

# MIND OVER MATTER

*Bodily exercise profits a little, but godliness is profitable for all things, having promise of the life that now is and of that which is to come.*

1 TIMOTHY 4:8 NKJV

As you look toward the New Year, you will probably think about your goals and aspirations. And one of those goals is likely to exercise more! We know the value of exercise; it benefits the body and the mind. We also know that exercise requires determination and discipline.

There is, however, exercise that is more beneficial than physical exercise. Scripture compares godliness with bodily exercise. Godliness is not just something that we instantly receive when we accept Christ as our Savior. Godliness is a work in progress. It requires discipline and commitment to understanding what it means to be like Jesus.

*Do you accept that you are going to have to put in the time and effort to prioritize spiritual practices in the same way you try to with physical exercise?*

God, I know that godliness has benefit beyond this life. Help me to be encouraged by your promises that make it clear that I will be rewarded in the life to come.

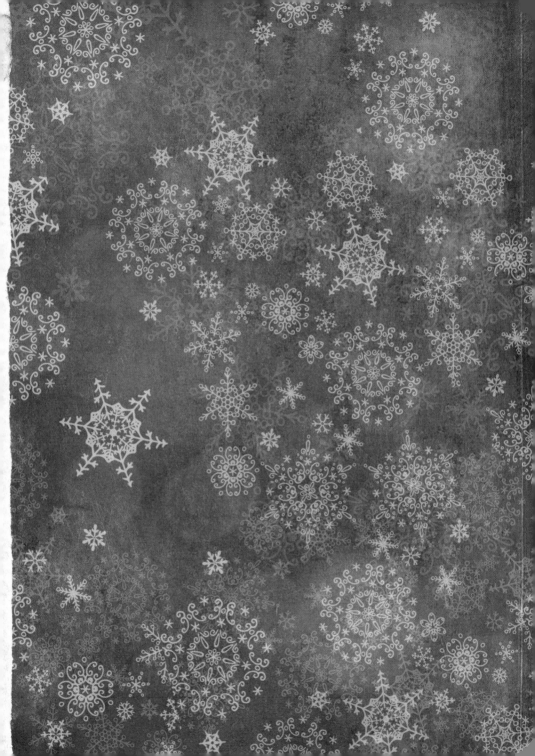